HOW THE HUMAN BODY WORKS

The Digestive System

By Simon Rose

MEDIA ENHANCED BOOKS

AV2 BY WEIGL™

ADDED VALUE • AUDIO VISUAL

www.av2books.com

MEDIA ENHANCED BOOKS

AV² BY WEIGL™

ADDED VALUE • AUDIO VISUAL

AV² provides enriched content that supplements and complements this book. Weigl's AV² books strive to create inspired learning and engage young minds in a total learning experience.

Your AV² Media Enhanced books come alive with...

Audio
Listen to sections of the book read aloud.

Key Words
Study vocabulary, and complete a matching word activity.

Go to **www.av2books.com**, and enter this book's unique code.

Video
Watch informative video clips.

Quizzes
Test your knowledge.

BOOK CODE

D 2 7 3 2 2 2

Embedded Weblinks
Gain additional information for research.

Slide Show
View images and captions, and prepare a presentation.

AV² by Weigl brings you media enhanced books that support active learning.

Try This!
Complete activities and hands-on experiments.

... and much, much more!

Published by AV² by Weigl
350 5th Avenue, 59th Floor
New York, NY 10118
Websites: www.av2books.com   www.weigl.com

Library of Congress Cataloging-in-Publication Data Available on Request

ISBN 978-1-4896-1166-6 (hardcover)
ISBN 978-1-4896-1167-3 (softcover)
ISBN 978-1-4896-1168-0 (single-user eBook)
ISBN 978-1-4896-1169-7 (multi-user eBook)

Printed in the United States of America in North Mankato, Minnesota
1 2 3 4 5 6 7 8 9 0 18 17 16 15 14

062014
WEP090514

Project Coordinator Aaron Carr
Art Director Terry Paulhus

Photo Credits
Every reasonable effort has been made to trace ownership and to obtain permission to reprint copyright material. The publishers would be pleased to have any errors or omissions brought to their attention so that they may be corrected in subsequent printings.

Weigl acknowledges Getty Images as its primary image supplier for this title.

Contents

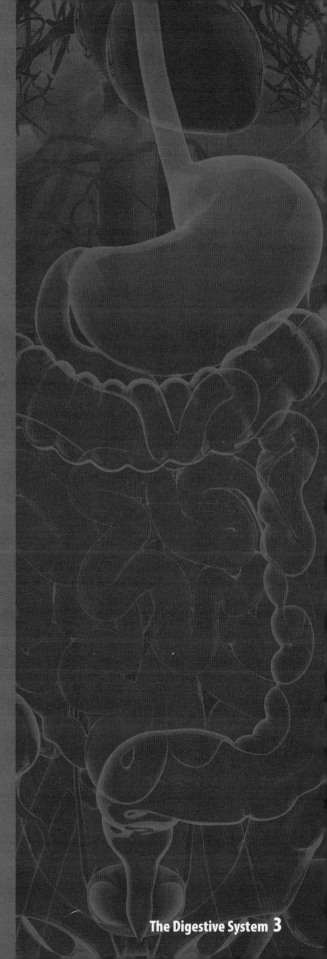

Human Body Systems

The human body is made up of many complex systems. Each one plays an important role in how the body works. However, the systems are also interconnected and function together.

The systems all need to work together properly. This helps the body stay healthy. A disease or disorder in one of the body's systems may involve not just that system. It can also have an effect on one or more of the other systems.

6 MAJOR BODY SYSTEMS

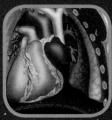

CARDIOVASCULAR SYSTEM

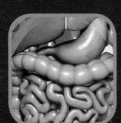

DIGESTIVE SYSTEM

MUSCULAR SYSTEM

NERVOUS SYSTEM

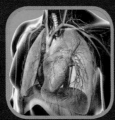

RESPIRATORY SYSTEM

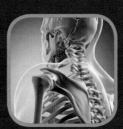

SKELETAL SYSTEM

DIGESTIVE SYSTEM

Is made up of a long tube that starts at the mouth

Contains several **organs**, including the esophagus, stomach, liver, pancreas, and intestines

Begins working as soon as food enters the mouth

Helps to convert food into nutrients, substances needed by the body to stay healthy

Helps to remove waste products from the body

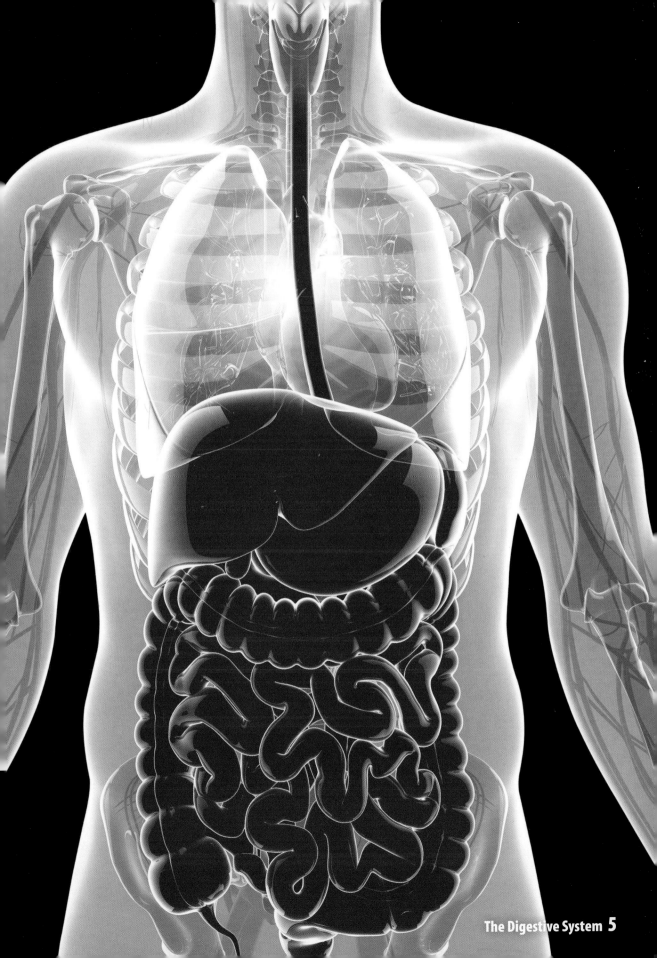

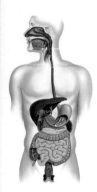

What Is the Digestive System?

The digestive system consists of the parts of the body that work together to convert, or change, the foods and liquids that are consumed into nutrients. The system also works to turn food that is not used into waste material. This waste is then removed from the body.

A long, twisting tube called the digestive tract passes through the body. This tube is also called the gastrointestinal tract or alimentary canal. The tube is made up of a number of different organs. Some are hollow, such as the mouth, esophagus, stomach, small intestine, and large intestine. Some of the organs are not hollow, such as the liver, pancreas, and gallbladder. The digestive tract extends from the mouth to the anus, where waste leaves the body. As food moves down the tract and through its parts, it is broken down into smaller pieces. It is also changed by acids and other substances produced by parts of the digestive system.

The body uses nutrients for growth and energy.

30 FEET

(9.1 meters) is the average length of the adult digestive system.

It takes more than **2 DAYS** to completely digest food, from eating to elimination from the body.

MORE THAN 400

different types of bacteria can be found in the intestines.

90%

of digestion takes place in the small intestine.

After a large meal, the adult stomach may hold

64

fluid ounces (1.9 liters).

The average American eats

1,996 pounds

(905 kilograms) of food each year.

In **7** seconds, food travels from the mouth, down the esophagus, and into the stomach.

Digestive System Features

The food people eat provides energy, vitamins, and minerals. The body, however, cannot use food in its original form. Once it enters the body, food must be broken down by the digestive system into materials that the different organs and **tissues** can use.

SALIVARY GLANDS These **glands**, which produce the liquid saliva, are found in and around the mouth, jaw, and throat.

PHARYNX This passageway goes from the mouth to the esophagus.

ESOPHAGUS This tube connects the pharynx to the stomach.

LIVER Found to the right of the stomach, the liver plays many different roles in the body.

GALLBLADDER This small, pear-shaped pouch is found under the liver.

PANCREAS This gland is located below and slightly behind the stomach. It secretes, or gives out, substances called enzymes that help with digestion.

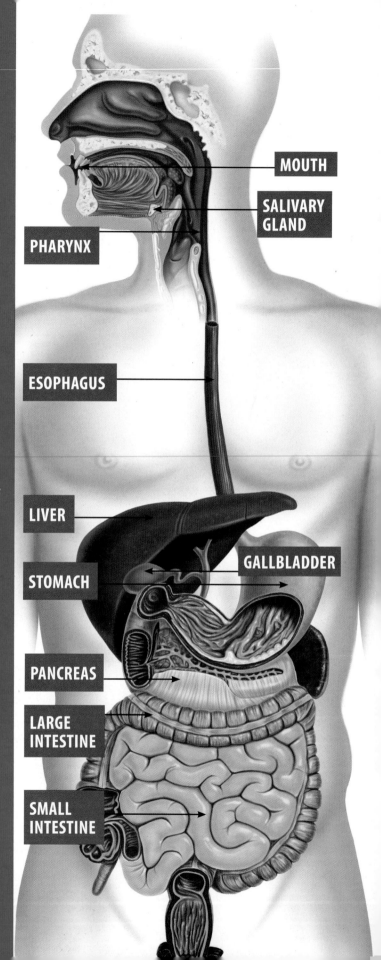

MOUTH

SALIVARY GLAND

PHARYNX

ESOPHAGUS

LIVER

GALLBLADDER

STOMACH

PANCREAS

LARGE INTESTINE

SMALL INTESTINE

Mouth

Also known as the oral cavity, this is where food begins the journey through the digestive system. Teeth are located on the sides and in the front of the mouth. There are also different muscles that help move food along.

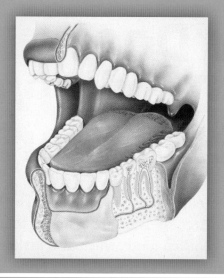

Stomach

The stomach is one of the most important parts of the digestive system. A rounded organ, shaped like a letter J, it is found in the left side of the abdomen, the part of the body between the chest and the pelvis. The stomach acts as a storage tank, holding food so that the body has enough time to digest properly.

Small Intestine

The small intestine is actually longer than the large intestine. It twists and turns and is packed into the abdomen under the stomach. When food enters the small intestine, it is in a semi-solid form. By the time the small intestine completes its work, the parts of food the body can use have become liquid.

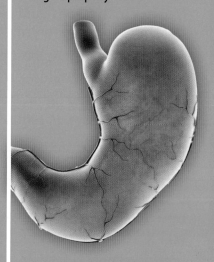

Large Intestine

The large intestine is a muscular tube that begins in the lower right part of the abdomen and travels up the right side. Then, it moves across to the left before it goes down the left side of the abdomen. The large intestine is one of the final parts of the digestive system.

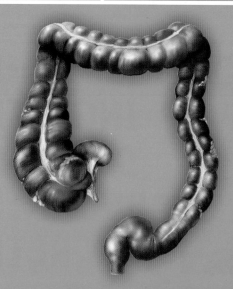

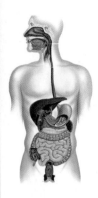

How Does the Digestive System Work?

Digestion begins in the mouth when food is chewed by the teeth. The smaller pieces that are produced are easier to swallow. Saliva in the mouth helps to moisten food, which also makes swallowing it easier. Saliva contains an enzyme that breaks down some of the **carbohydrates** in food.

Muscles in the throat and esophagus push the food down to the stomach. This is done by a series of muscular contractions called peristalsis. Another tube called the windpipe, or trachea, leads from the throat to the lungs. When a person swallows, a small flap of tissue known as the epiglottis prevents food and liquid from traveling to the lungs. Instead, they enter the esophagus, where digestion continues.

Food then reaches the stomach, which produces and secretes gastric juices. These contain **mucus**, a type of acid, and various enzymes. The enzymes break down **proteins**. The contents of the stomach then move to the small intestine, where peristalsis also takes place. This helps to move the food and mix it with various secretions from the liver and pancreas. These secretions break down food further. At this point, nutrients move from the small intestine into the blood, which carries them throughout the body.

The Role of the Digestive System

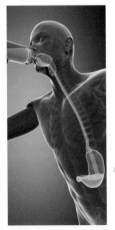

INGESTION Food is taken in and broken down.

SECRETION Fluids and enzymes are produced and secreted to help digest food.

ABSORPTION Nutrients are absorbed by, or taken into, the body from the small intestine.

EXCRETION The digestive system disposes of waste.

Diagram of Layers of the Digestive Tract

The digestive tract has four layers. The outermost layer, the serosa, is made of loose **connective tissue**. This makes the tract strong. The next layer is the muscularis externa. It includes two layers of muscle. They enable the digestive tract to move and make peristalsis possible. The third layer is the submucosa. Connective tissue and **blood vessels** are found there. The inner layer is the mucosa, which contains special cells called epithelial cells. The mucosa also has muscles, which help move food, and connective tissue, which keeps structures in position.

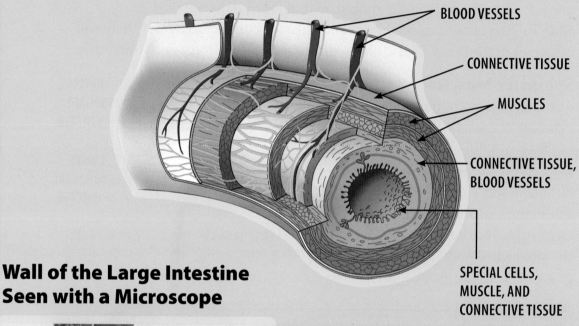

BLOOD VESSELS

CONNECTIVE TISSUE

MUSCLES

CONNECTIVE TISSUE, BLOOD VESSELS

SPECIAL CELLS, MUSCLE, AND CONNECTIVE TISSUE

Wall of the Large Intestine Seen with a Microscope

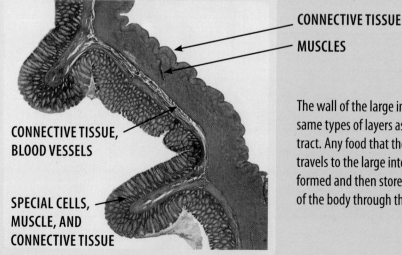

CONNECTIVE TISSUE

MUSCLES

CONNECTIVE TISSUE, BLOOD VESSELS

SPECIAL CELLS, MUSCLE, AND CONNECTIVE TISSUE

The wall of the large intestine is made up of the same types of layers as the rest of the digestive tract. Any food that the body is not able to use travels to the large intestine. There, feces are formed and then stored until they are sent out of the body through the rectum and anus.

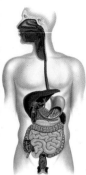

The Mouth and Neck

Adults have 32 permanent teeth set in the upper and lower jaw of the mouth. Teeth are made of a hard, bone-like substance called dentin and covered with a layer of enamel. There are nerves and blood vessels under the dentin.

The tongue contains a number of muscles. The outside of the tongue has small bumps that grip food as it is moved by the muscles. The muscles move food to the back of the mouth so that it can be swallowed. In addition, the taste buds on the tongue's surface connect to nerves that send messages to the brain. These give sensations of sweet, sour, salty, and bitter.

Sphincter Muscles

At the upper end of the esophagus is a bundle of muscles called the upper esophageal sphincter. It closes after food enters the esophagus. Another bundle of muscles, the lower esophageal sphincter, is at the lower end of the esophagus. It closes after food enters the stomach. This keeps food from going back up the esophagus.

When the upper esophageal sphincter closes, it prevents food from moving up out of the esophagus and going down the trachea.

UPPER ESOPHAGEAL SPHINCTER

LOWER ESOPHAGEAL SPHINCTER

ESOPHAGUS →

— STOMACH

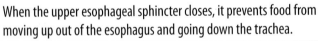

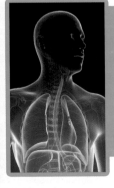

The MOUTH AND NECK by the Numbers

¼	3	8
The epiglottis in an adult is ¼ inch (0.6 centimeters) in length.	There are three groups of salivary glands in and around the mouth.	An adult's esophagus is 8 inches (20 cm) long.

Diagram of the Mouth and Neck

The parts of the digestive system in the mouth and neck are used to get food inside the body. They also begin the process of breaking the food down. Teeth have different shapes so they can handle food in specific ways. Some teeth are shaped to bite off large pieces. Others grasp and tear food. Still others grind food.

The Mouth

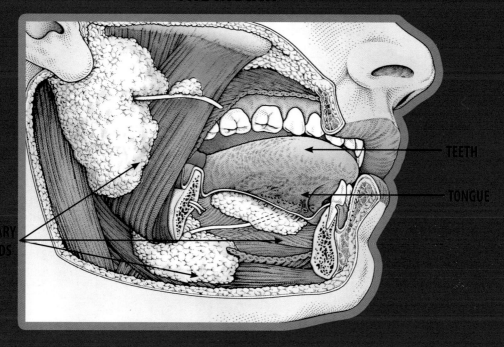

TEETH

TONGUE

SALIVARY GLANDS

Teeth

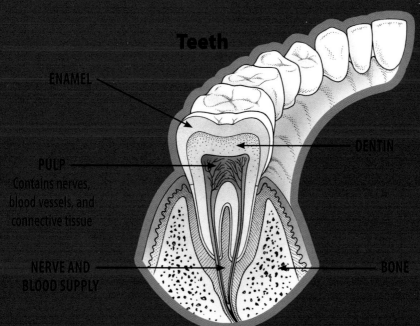

ENAMEL

DENTIN

PULP
Contains nerves, blood vessels, and connective tissue

NERVE AND BLOOD SUPPLY

BONE

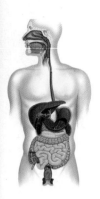

The Stomach

The stomach can expand, or become larger, depending on the amount of food it contains. The stomach can hold a great deal of food. This means people have to eat only a few times a day.

The stomach's inner layer is covered with folds, or wrinkles, of muscle tissue. These folds make it possible for the stomach to stretch, which lets the stomach hold more food. The folds also help to grip and move food during the digestive process.

Acids and Enzymes

While food is in the stomach, it mixes with acids and enzymes that the stomach secretes. The food is processed into a thick, semi-liquid paste called chyme. At the lower end of the stomach is a muscle called the pyloric sphincter. This keeps the chyme in the stomach until it is ready to be passed into the small intestine.

Without the stomach's ability to hold food, people would have to eat constantly.

The STOMACH by the Numbers

6.3	12	2–5
The stomach produces 6.3 pints (3 L) of acid every day.	The average length of an adult stomach is 12 inches (30 cm).	Food stays in the stomach for two to five hours.

Diagram of the Stomach

While food is held in the stomach, the digestive process that began in the mouth and esophagus continues. Food is prepared for further digestion in the small intestine. This further digestion is helped by the liver, gallbladder, and pancreas.

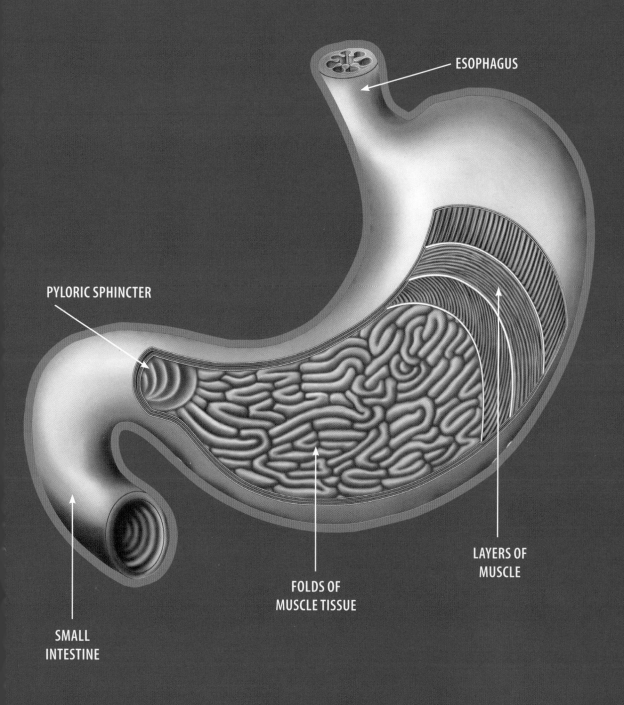

ESOPHAGUS

PYLORIC SPHINCTER

LAYERS OF MUSCLE

FOLDS OF MUSCLE TISSUE

SMALL INTESTINE

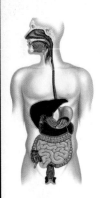

The Liver, Gallbladder, and Pancreas

The liver is the second-largest organ and the largest gland in the body. It has two lobes, or sections. The left lobe is smaller and flatter than the right lobe. Without the liver, the body's tissues would not receive the nutrients and energy they need. Blood traveling from the small intestine goes to the liver, which processes the nutrients before the blood delivers them to different parts of the body. The liver also breaks down unwanted chemicals, so that they can be passed from the body as waste.

The liver produces a fluid called bile. Bile helps with digestion by breaking down fats into **fatty acids**. Bile is stored in the gallbladder, located next to the liver. When bile is needed, muscle contractions cause the gallbladder to send it to the small intestine.

The pancreas is a gland that secretes digestive enzymes into the small intestine. They help to digest foods by breaking down proteins, fats, carbohydrates, and **nucleic acids**. The pancreas also produces a hormone called insulin.

Insulin produced by the pancreas processes sugar in the body.

The LIVER, GALLBLADDER, AND PANCREAS by the Numbers

3
An adult's liver weighs about 3 pounds (1.4 kg).

50.7
Each day, the pancreas secretes 50.7 fluid ounces (1.5 L) of liquid.

3
The average gallbladder is 3 inches (7.6 cm) long.

Diagram of the Liver, Gallbladder, and Pancreas

The liver, gallbladder, and pancreas are not just involved with digestion. They also play other roles in the body. The liver, for example, makes proteins that help with blood **clotting**.

Liver and Other Organs

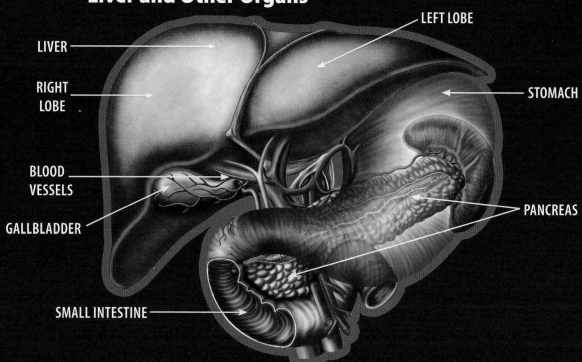

LEFT LOBE

LIVER

RIGHT LOBE

STOMACH

BLOOD VESSELS

GALLBLADDER

PANCREAS

SMALL INTESTINE

Pancreas and Gallbladder

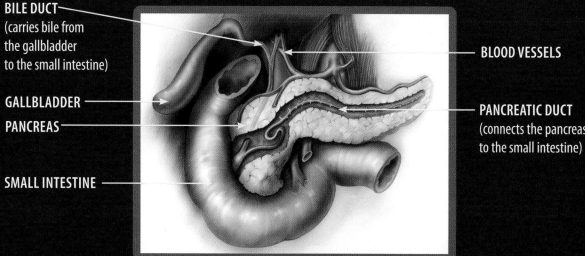

BILE DUCT
(carries bile from the gallbladder to the small intestine)

BLOOD VESSELS

GALLBLADDER

PANCREAS

PANCREATIC DUCT
(connects the pancreas to the small intestine)

SMALL INTESTINE

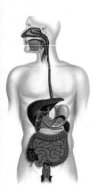

The Intestines

The small and large intestine make up a long, continuous tube that runs from the stomach to the anus. The small intestine is coiled like a hose inside the body. It has three main sections. The first, the duodenum, receives chemicals and partially digested food from the stomach. In the second part, the jejunum, most of the nutrients removed from food during digestion are absorbed into the blood. The remaining nutrients are absorbed in the last part, the ileum. Waste that remains moves into the large intestine.

The Colon

The large intestine is also known as the colon. It is about 5 feet (1.5 m) long and 2.5 inches (6.3 cm) wide. The large intestine does not break down food. Its major role is to remove water from food that has not been digested. The water is absorbed into the body, and solid feces are formed.

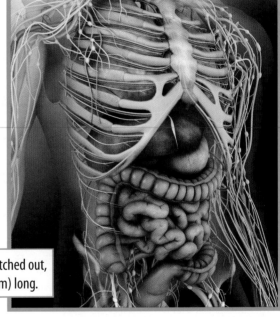

If an adult's small intestine were stretched out, it would measure about 22 feet (6.7 m) long.

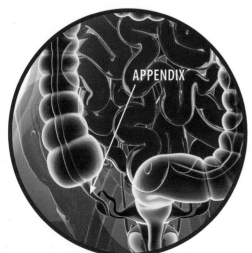

APPENDIX

THE APPENDIX

A narrow pouch of tissue called the appendix is attached to the large intestine. Scientists are not sure what role it plays in the body. Doctors remove the appendix if it becomes infected.

Diagram of the Intestines

Together, the small and large intestine take up the majority of the area inside the abdomen. About 2.5 gallons (9.5 L) of food, liquids, and waste are processed by the intestines every day.

Small Intestine

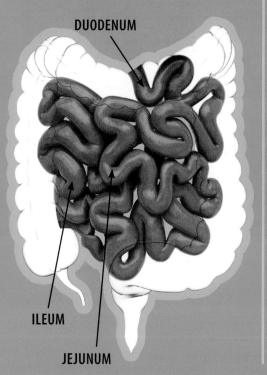

DUODENUM

ILEUM

JEJUNUM

Large Intestine

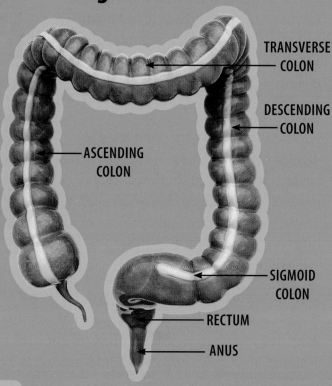

TRANSVERSE COLON

DESCENDING COLON

ASCENDING COLON

SIGMOID COLON

RECTUM

ANUS

VILLI   BLOOD VESSELS

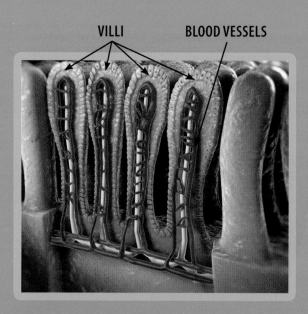

INTESTINAL WALL

The inside surface of the small intestine is covered with millions of tiny structures called villi. They enlarge the surface area of the small intestine. This greatly increases the amounts of nutrients that can be absorbed into the blood.

Keeping Healthy

I f the digestive system is damaged or is not working properly, the body will not receive the nutrients it needs. It will also not be able to rid itself of waste products. Having a healthful lifestyle, eating the right foods, and getting regular exercise are all important in keeping the digestive system working at its best.

Healthful Diet

Foods rich in **fiber** are good for the digestive system. These include vegetables, fruits, and whole-grain bread, cereal, or pasta. The protein contained in eggs, fish, beans, nuts, poultry, and other types of meat is also good for digestion. Water is important for a healthy digestive system as well.

People should be careful about not eating too much fat, which can upset the digestive system.

It is always best not to eat too much. Overeating puts stress on the digestive system. Food should be well chewed, so that it is easier to swallow. This means people should not eat in a hurry. In addition, meals should not be skipped.

HIGH IN FIBER

A slice of whole-wheat bread has 1.9 grams of fiber. A banana has 3.1 grams, a cup of peas has 8 grams, and a cup of black beans has 15 grams.

Exercise

Regular exercise is good for the digestive system. About 30 minutes of exercise at least three times a week is helpful. Exercise helps muscles in the intestines work properly.

Exercise can strengthen the muscles of the abdomen.

Digestive System Diseases

Celiac disease is caused by an abnormal response of the **immune system** to gluten. This is a protein found in wheat, barley, and rye. When someone with celiac disease eats gluten, it causes inflammation in the small intestine. This can damage the intestine and prevent some nutrients from being absorbed. People with celiac disease can follow a special gluten-free diet.

38 GRAMS

The amount of fiber an adult man should eat every day. A woman should eat 25 grams.

Irritable bowel syndrome (IBS) affects the colon. People with IBS may have abdominal cramps, constipation, and diarrhea. IBS has no cure, but the condition can be managed by changes in diet and lifestyle. Sometimes, medications are also used.

Peptic ulcers are sores that develop on the inside of the stomach, esophagus, or upper part of the small intestine. They happen when acid in the digestive tract wears away the inner surface of an organ. Peptic ulcers can usually be treated with medication.

WAIT A WHILE

It is best not to exercise right after eating a full meal.

Studying the Digestive System

Today, several types of medical professionals study and treat diseases of the digestive system. These professionals are usually specialists in an area of modern medicine. However, people have been studying the digestive system since ancient times.

EARLY STUDY

1550 BC In ancient Egypt, the Ebers Papyrus describes various medical conditions and details about the human body and its systems.

About 460 to 375 BC

The Greek physician Hippocrates, called the "father of medicine," spends much of his life studying the human body.

Early 1500s AD

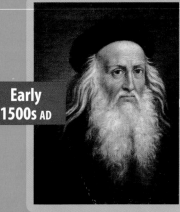

The Italian artist and scientist Leonardo da Vinci creates hundreds of drawings in a detailed study of human anatomy.

Physician Burrill B. Crohn publishes a scientific paper identifying the intestinal disorder that later becomes known as Crohn's disease.

1932

1950s

Dutch physician Willem-Karel Dicke identifies gluten as the cause of celiac disease and develops the gluten-free diet.

1969

The first colonoscopy is performed by doctors, who use an endoscope to view the large intestine and remove growths from it.

The Italian biologist Lazzaro Spallanzani publishes the results of experiments on the role of gastric juices in digestion.

1780

1761

Giovanni Morgagni, a professor in Padua, Italy, studies many aspects of the body, including the digestive system, and publishes *On the Sites and Causes of Diseases*.

After Alexis St. Martin is shot in the stomach, surgeon William Beaumont saves his life. A fistula, or hole, is left in St. Martin's abdominal wall. Beaumont conducts tests on St. Martin's digestive system in the following years.

1822

1868

German physician Adolf Kussmaul uses an endoscope to examine the inside of a living person's stomach for the first time.

1853

Antoine Jean Desormeaux develops the endoscope, a lighted tube with mirrors, to examine internal organs.

In London, England, the first CAT scan, which stands for computed axial tomography, is performed on a patient's brain. CAT scans are now used to examine a number of body parts.

1972

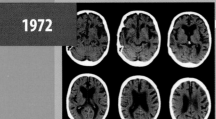

2005

Barry Marshall and Robin Warren are awarded a Nobel Prize for their discovery of the bacterium that causes **gastritis** and peptic ulcer disease.

Working Together

All the systems in the body must work together to keep people healthy. The digestive system, for example, provides the rest of the body with the nutrients that are needed to maintain health and life. The digestive system works closely with several other systems of the body.

Nutrients and the Blood

The digestive system works with the circulatory system to send nutrients that have been absorbed around the body. Some of these nutrients are delivered by blood vessels to tissues in the organs of the digestive system itself. These organs, just like all other parts of the body, need to receive nutrients in order to function.

A person should drink
8–12
8-ounce glasses (2–3 L) of water and other liquids per day.

Water the body needs is absorbed into the blood from the small intestine.

Digestion and the Nervous System

The nervous system plays a role in eating and drinking by controlling the parts of the muscular system that help people to chew, swallow, and eliminate waste. It also determines how quickly food moves through the digestive system. The operation of internal organs, including the stomach and intestines, is controlled by the autonomic nervous system.

The actions caused by the autonomic nervous system are involuntary. This means that they happen without people thinking about them. As a result, people often are not aware that internal organs are working when food moves through the stomach or intestines.

Nerves throughout the body play a role in digestion. Some nerves, for example, stimulate digestion by increasing blood flow to the digestive tract.

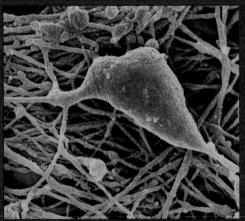

More Than One

Two different types of nerves help control the action of the digestive system. Extrinsic nerves cause muscles to contract, in order to push food along the digestive tract. Intrinsic nerves are found inside the walls of the esophagus, stomach, and intestines. These nerves release substances that slow down or speed up the movement of food and the production of digestive juices.

Doctors and other health-care workers specialize in treating digestive system problems. Many of these careers require studying science, especially biology. A desire to work with people is also helpful. Before considering any type of career, it is important to research options and learn about the educational requirements.

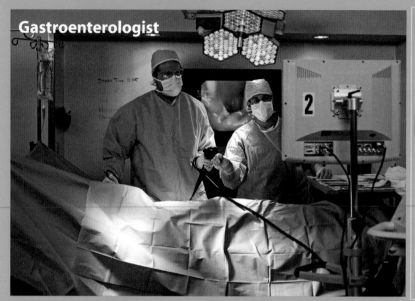

Gastroenterologist

Education

- College and MD degrees
- Residency program
- Advanced training

Tools

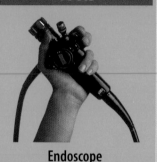

Endoscope

Gastroenterologists are doctors who specialize in diseases of the digestive system. They diagnose and treat medical conditions that affect organs such as the stomach, intestines, and esophagus. Gastroenterologists examine patients and carry out tests by such methods as endoscopy. They also provide patients with advice and information about avoiding digestive diseases and dealing with them if they occur.

Education

To become a gastroenterologist, a person must graduate from college and then attend medical school for four years to earn an MD (doctor of medicine) degree. After this comes a three-year program of special study, called a residency, in internal medicine. Gastroenterologists then spend two or three years in an advanced training program studying diseases of the digestive tract and their treatment.

Hepatology is a specialized area of gastroenterology. Hepatologists diagnose and treat medical conditions of the liver and related organs, such as the gallbladder and pancreas. They perform different medical examinations and tests such as **biopsies** and endoscopies.

Education

To become a hepatologist, a person must graduate from college and then receive an MD degree. This is followed by a residency in internal medicine. Most hepatologists then undergo additional training.

Hepatologist

Education

- College and MD degrees
- Residency program
- Advanced training

Tools

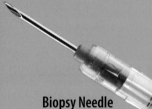

Biopsy Needle

Medical imaging technologists operate equipment, such as MRI, X-ray, and **ultrasound** machines. These technologists produce the images that allow medical professionals to see internal body parts. Technologists provide doctors with information needed to diagnose and treat illnesses.

Education

Technologists can attend different types of schools. Many attend a two-year program. They need to pass a test to get a license and must take courses to keep their skills up-to-date.

Medical Imaging Technologist

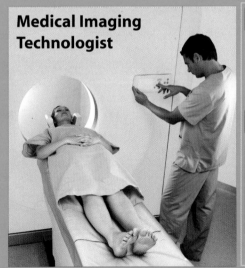

Education

- Two-year degree
- Special training
- Licensing exam

Tools

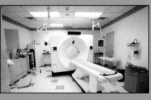

MRI Machine

The Digestive System Quiz

Test your knowledge of the digestive system by answering these questions. The answers are provided below for easy reference.

1 What is the name for a thick semi-liquid paste produced in the stomach?

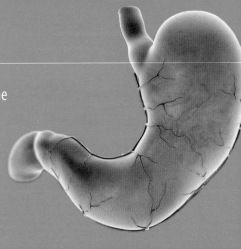

4 What do hepatologists specialize in?

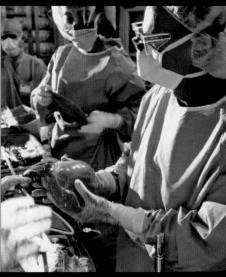

7 What is the first part of the small intestine called?

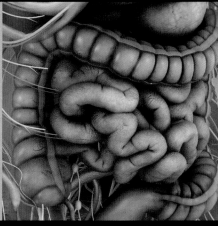

8 What is the largest gland in the body?

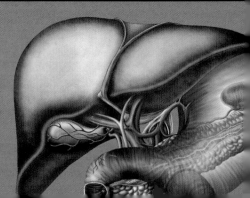

2 Who first developed the endoscope in 1853?

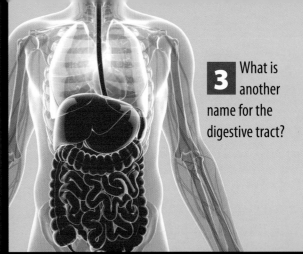

3 What is another name for the digestive tract?

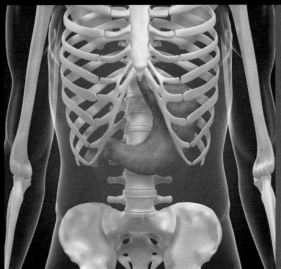

5 What is the average length of the adult digestive system?

6 About how much material can an adult's stomach hold after a large meal?

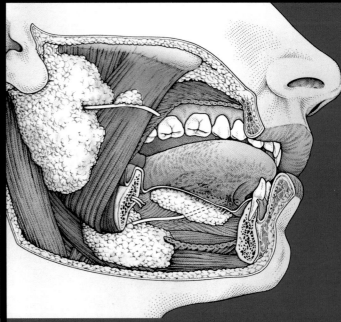

9 Celiac disease is caused by an abnormal response to what substance?

10 How many groups of salivary glands are located in and around the mouth?

Activity

The stomach is somewhat like an electric mixer. It breaks down food, converting solid substances into liquids. You can get an idea of how this works by using common foods and household objects.

BEFORE YOU START, YOU WILL NEED:

2 zip-lock sandwich bags
A few crackers
1 spoonful of water
2 ounces (60 ml) of orange juice

How the Stomach Works

1 Put the crackers into one of the zip-lock bags. Seal the bag shut.

2 Use your fingers to break up the crackers in the bag. Note that this is similar to the way teeth begin digestion in the mouth.

3 Open the bag and pour the water in. The water represents saliva. What differences do you see in the crackers now? In your mouth, pieces of food that are moistened by saliva can be pushed by the tongue into the esophagus.

4 Think about what happens when food enters the stomach. It interacts with stomach acids. Open the bag again. Add the orange juice, which represents the acids.

5 Squeeze the contents of the bag for about two minutes. This is similar to the way the stomach muscles churn and process food to break it down. If your bag begins to leak, place it and all of its contents into the second zip-lock bag.

6 Look at the contents of the bag or bags. The food should have become liquid. In the stomach, the food would now be in the correct state to be sent to the small intestine.

Key Words

biopsies: medical tests that involve removing tissues or cells from the body and examining them for signs of disease

blood vessels: tube-shaped structures, such as arteries, veins, and capillaries, that carry blood around the body

carbohydrates: substances found in foods such as bread and potatoes that provide the body with energy

clotting: when blood forms a thick mass, changing from liquid form to solid

connective tissue: the parts of the body that support and hold together muscles, organs, and bones

fatty acids: the building blocks of fats in the body, formed when the body breaks down fats in food

fiber: plant material that the body cannot digest

gastritis: inflammation or swelling of the lining of the stomach

glands: cells or organs that produce and release substances for use in the body

immune system: the body system that protects the body from germs and other harmful substances

mucus: a thick liquid produced by certain parts of the body

nucleic acids: types of acids found in living cells

organs: parts of the body that perform special functions

proteins: substances found in foods such as eggs, meat, fish, and nuts that are important for the health and growth of body tissues

tissues: structures in the body made up of the same type of cells, which are the smallest units in living things that can perform the functions necessary for life

ultrasound: examination of structures inside the body using sound waves to create images

Index

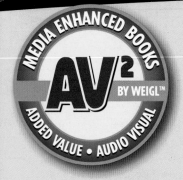

Log on to www.av2books.com

AV[2] by Weigl brings you media enhanced books that support active learning. Go to www.av2books.com, and enter the special code found on page 2 of this book. You will gain access to enriched and enhanced content that supplements and complements this book. Content includes video, audio, weblinks, quizzes, a slide show, and activities.

AV[2] Online Navigation

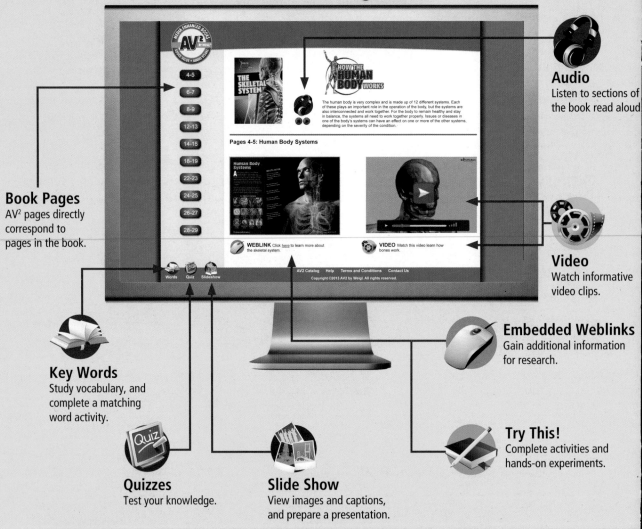

Book Pages
AV[2] pages directly correspond to pages in the book.

Audio
Listen to sections of the book read aloud

Video
Watch informative video clips.

Key Words
Study vocabulary, and complete a matching word activity.

Embedded Weblinks
Gain additional information for research.

Try This!
Complete activities and hands-on experiments.

Quizzes
Test your knowledge.

Slide Show
View images and captions, and prepare a presentation.

AV[2] was built to bridge the gap between print and digital. We encourage you to tell us what you like and what you want to see in the future.

Sign up to be an AV[2] Ambassador at www.av2books.com/ambassador.